Mel Bay's
VIOLIN METHOD

BY FRANK ZUCCO

The Mel Bay *Violin Method* is a modern approach, teaching sound fundamentals of violin performance. We recommend the following books as supplements to this method:

Building Excellence Series/Easy Solos for Beginning Violin
Building Excellence Series/Technical Studies for Beginning Violin
Building Excellence Series/Rhythmic Studies for Beginning Violin
Kidfiddle (solos)
EZ Way Fiddle Solos
Easy Violin Duets in 1st Position
Handbook for Violin Students (overall technical studies)
Solo Pieces for the Beginning Violinist

A B C D E F G
LA SI (DO) RE MI FA SOL

THE VIOLIN AND ITS PARTS

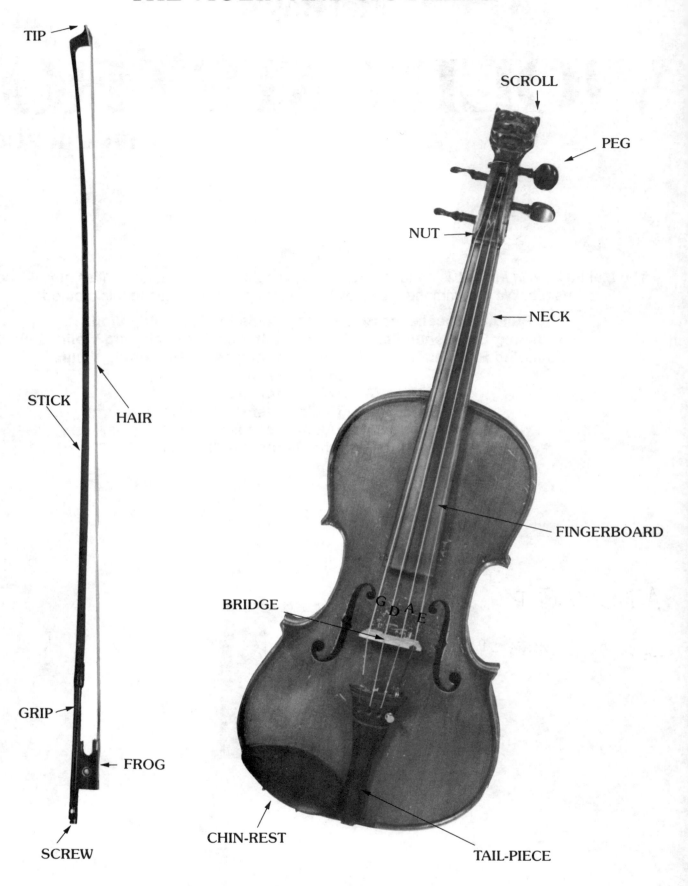

TIP

STICK

HAIR

GRIP

FROG

SCREW

SCROLL

PEG

NUT

NECK

FINGERBOARD

BRIDGE

G D A E

CHIN-REST

TAIL-PIECE

HOW TO HOLD THE VIOLIN

3 The first thing we will do in learning how to hold the violin is to grasp it with our left hand on the left shoulder of the instrument.

4 Hold the violin at arms length to get a feeling for the weight of the instrument and to prepare for placing it under the chin.

5 Turn the violin upside down in preparation for placement under chin.

6 Next, place the violin between the chin and the shoulder. The body should remain still while bringing the violin in position underneath the chin. Figures 3, 4, 5 & 6 should be practiced in sequence to help the student gain a sure feeling for the instrument.

7 Look at Figure 7. Notive that the scroll of the violin is held high. (It should not droop downward.) Notice also that the left elbow is held away from the body. (Do not push your left elbow against your side!)

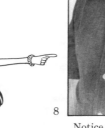

8 Notice in Figure 8 that the left elbow is held directly underneath the violin.

9 The violin should be positioned so that the student may look directly down the fingerboard as shown in Figure 9.

THE BOW

The bow like the violin, also comes in four sizes. Be sure to obtain the correct bow. Matching the bow and the violin is very important. Put rosin on the bow, a little each day. Never allow rosin, however, to collect on the violin or on the bow stick. Too much rosin tends to make the strings sound false. Always keep your strings clean. You might wipe them off with a soft cloth at the end of each practice period. The bow hair may be tightened or loosened by turning the screw at the end of the frog. Never tighten the bow too tight. This will cause your hair to break and the bow to warp when playing. The hair should be about 1/2″ away from the stick at the middle of the bow. Always loosen the hair when not playing. Remember, the tip of the bow goes into the small end of the case and the frog in to the large end. The bow, like the violin, is made of wood and is fragile. Dropping the bow can cause serious damage to it. Handle it with care.

HOW TO HOLD THE BOW

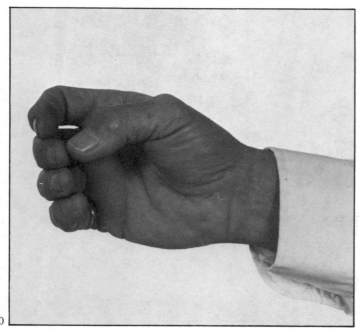

10

Hold your right hand with the thumb and second finger touching as shown in the photo.

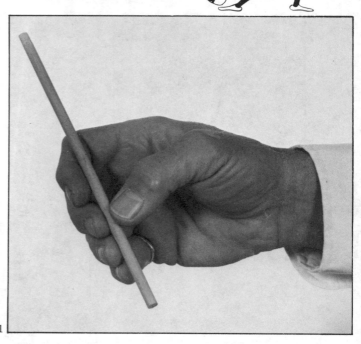

11

Using a pencil or stick, grasp as shown in the picture.

4

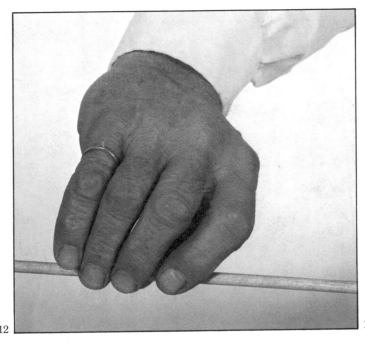

12

While grasping the pencil or stick, turn your hand over and make certain that your fingers rest gently on the object as shown in the Photo.

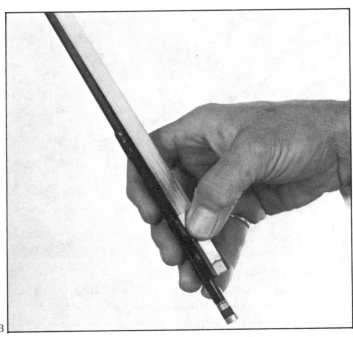

13

Now we are ready to pick up the bow.
Grasp the bow so that the thumb rests on the bottom of the frog. The other fingers are placed gently on the top of the bow.

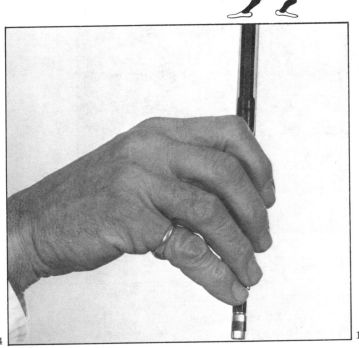

14

Turn your hand over and make certain that the bow is held as in the photo. Make certain that you do not grasp it too hard. Never allow your fingers to become stiff and rigid.

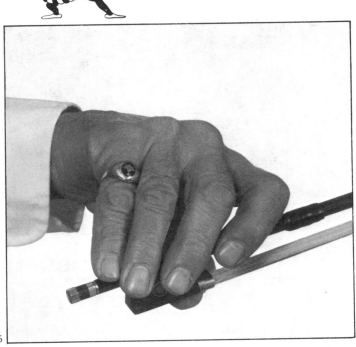

15

Note: The first finger should sit on the bow at the middle joint.

"BOWING" OR "DRAWING THE BOW"

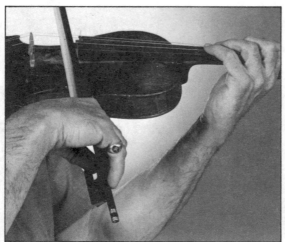

UP 16

DOWN BOW

Moving the bow from the tip to the frog is called up bow. The symbol for up bow is ∨.

| 17

DOWN

UP BOW

Drawing the bow from the frog to the tip is called Down Bow. The symbol for down bow is ⊓.

In order to bow in the proper manner, move only that part of the area from the elbow down.

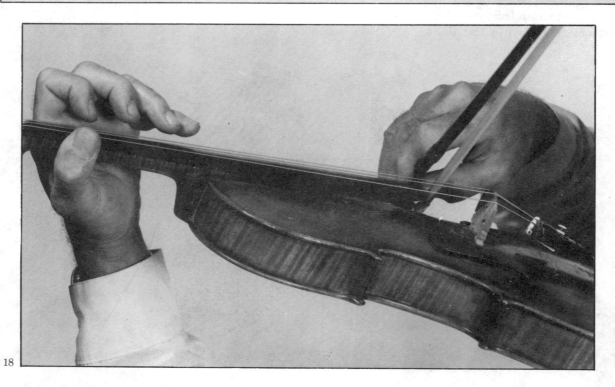

18

OUR FIRST TONE

We are now ready to play our first note on the violin. Make certain that you are holding the violin and the bow in the correct manner. Place your bow about one inch from the bridge of the violin and let it rest on the first or "E" string as shown above in Figure 18.

To play the first note, none of your left hand fingers should be touching any of the strings. As in Figure 18 above. Now, draw your bow down.

Make certain that you *draw the bow in a straight line* and with a steady manner.

This note that you are playing is called "E." It looks like this.

Draw your bow down and up, making a slight pause between each stroke. Keep repeating this down—up motion until the tone begins to become clear. After a good clear tone is achieved on the "E" string, try practicing this down—up bowing exercise on the remaining strings.

LEARNING ABOUT NOTES

SIDE VIEW

THIS IS OUR FIRST NOTE.

"E"

It represents the open "E" string. Open E, on the staff, is the same as the open E on the first string on the violin.

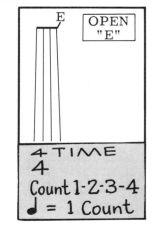

E

OPEN "E"

4 TIME
4
Count 1-2-3-4
♩ = 1 Count

FRONT VIEW

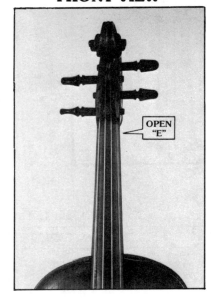

OPEN "E"

Quarter note
Black with stem
Gets one beat

Quarter rest
See a sea horse
Gets one beat

"G" Treble or Clef (handwritten)

QUARTER NOTE

HALF NOTE

Half note
Gets 2 beats
White with stem

ANOTHER NOTE

HALF REST

Half rest
Sits on the third line
Gets 2 beats

7

A STRING

Open A

The 2nd string is the A string.

THE LONG ONE

WHOLE NOTE

Whole note   o

Gets 4 beats   o

White·no stem   o

WHOLE REST

Whole rest

Hangs down from the fourth line and gets 4 beats.

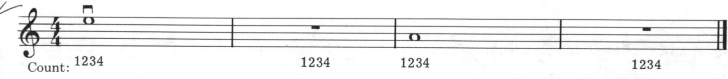

Count: 1234   1234   1234   1234

PLAY AND COUNT ALOUD

D STRING

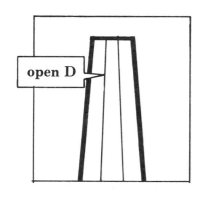

open D

The 3rd string is the D string.

I PLAY "D"

MIXER

MIXER #2

MORE

NOTE STUDY

TRY FOR GOOD SOUND

DOWN UP

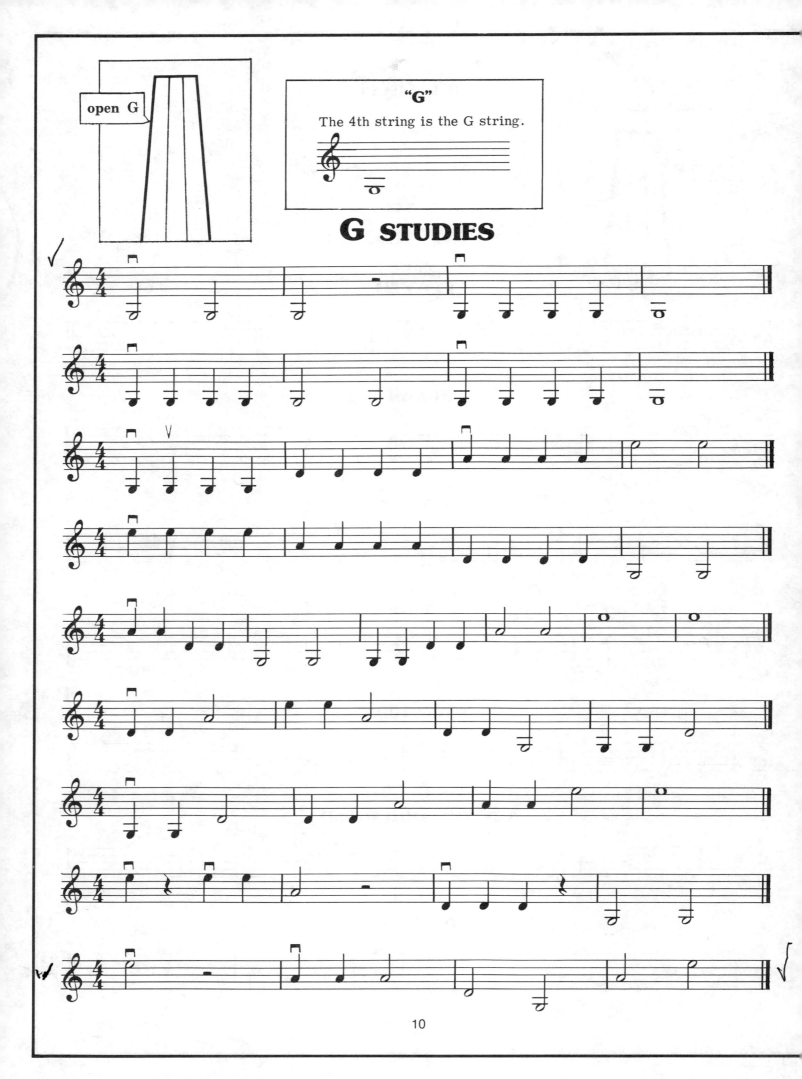

POSITIONING OF THE LEFT HAND

> *When playing the violin, the left hand should be positioned as shown in the photos below.*

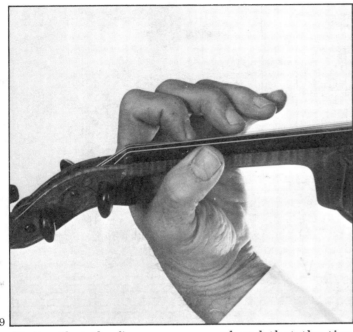

19

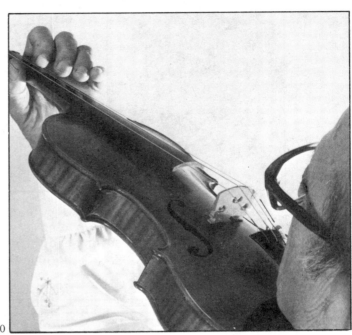

20

Notice that the fingers are curved and that the tips of the fingers press down the strings. Figures 19 and 20.

The thumb rests on the side of the neck. Figure 19.

The wrist is held straight (but not stiff) and away from the neck of the violin. Figure 19.

All fingers remain over the fingerboard. Figure 21.

Notice in Figure 22 the opening between the hand and the back of the neck. Palm of hand should never touch back of neck.

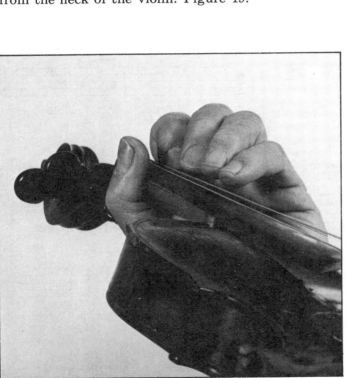

21

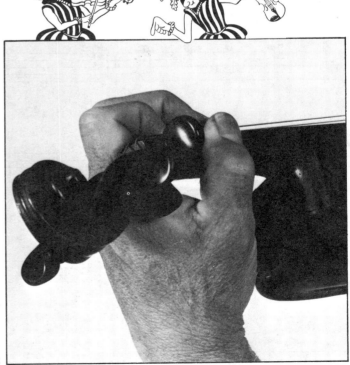

22

NOTES ON THE "E" STRING

SIDE VIEW

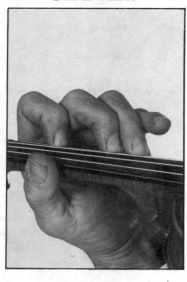

FRONT VIEW

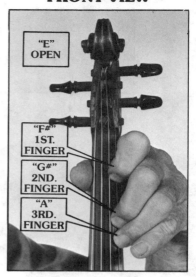

Notice the wide space between the first and second fingers (F#) and (G#) in the photograph. This wide spacing is called "whole step." Next, notice the small space between the second and third fingers (G#) and (A). This is called a half step. When playing "A", continue to hold the 1st and 2nd fingers down.

NOTES ON THE "A" STRING

FRONT VIEW

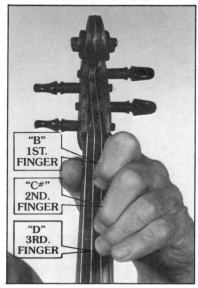

"B" 1ST. FINGER

"C#" 2ND. FINGER

"D" 3RD. FINGER

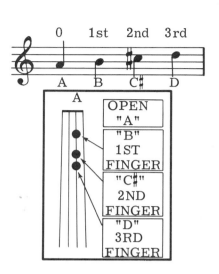

0   1st   2nd   3rd

A   B   C#   D

A	
	OPEN "A"
	"B" 1ST FINGER
	"C#" 2ND FINGER
	"D" 3RD FINGER

SIDE VIEW

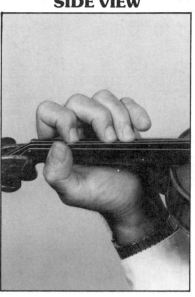

Notice that the spacing of the fingers for the notes on the A string is the same as on the E string. We have a whole step between the 1st and 2nd fingers and a 1/2 step between the 2nd and 3rd fingers. When playing "D", continue to hold the 1st and 2nd fingers down.

LET'S PLAY ALL THE NOTES ON THE "A" STRING

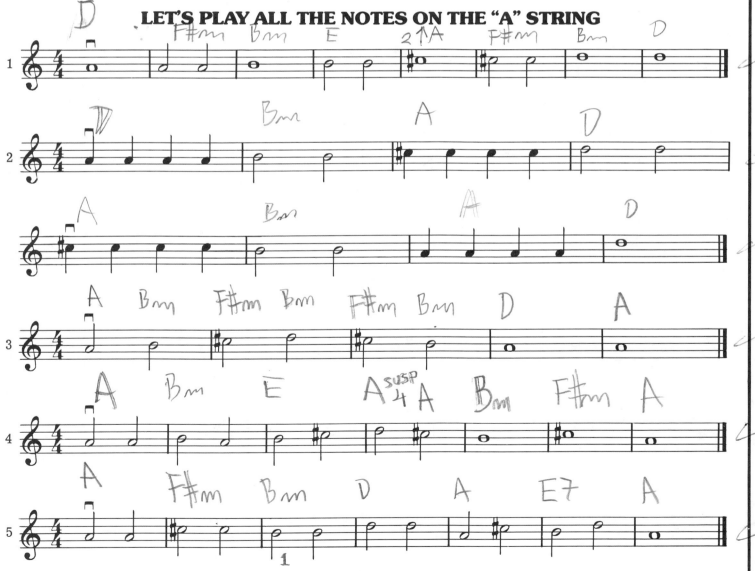

13

E AND A STRING COMBINED

AU CLAIR DE LA LUNE

French Song

AGAIN

OH WHEN THE SAINTS

Spiritual

HOW FIRM A FOUNDATION

Early American Hymn

THINGS TO REMEMBER

Study the illustrations carefully. We will not review the correct positioning of the left hand and fingers.

Wrong — Fingers curved back.

Correct — Fingers curved over strings.

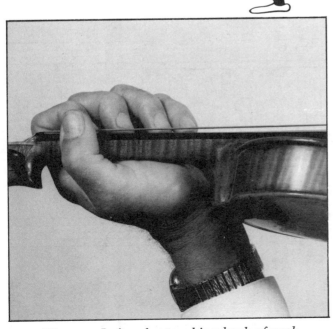

Wrong — Left palm touching back of neck.

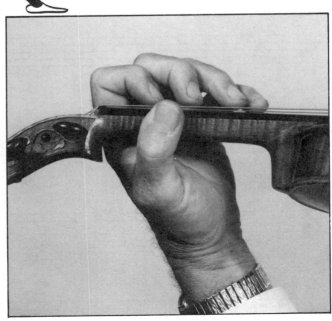

Correct — Position of palm and wrist.

THIRD STRING "D" STRING

FRONT VIEW

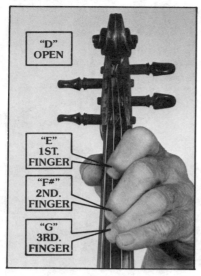

The position of the fingers on the "D" string is the same as on the "A" and "E" strings. To play the notes on the "D" string, however, it will be necessary to raise the right elbow (bow arm) slightly higher.

SIDE VIEW

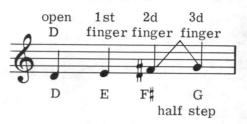

PLAY AND COMPARE

STUDIES

HAYDN'S SURPRISE

OH! SUSANNA

BUFFALO GALS

CHORALE (DUET)

FOURTH STRING "G" STRING

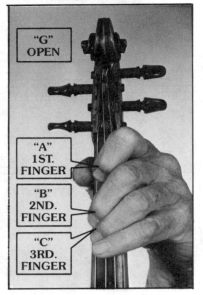

"G" OPEN

"A" 1ST. FINGER

"B" 2ND. FINGER

"C" 3RD. FINGER

The position of the fingers on the "G" string is the same as on the "E", "A", and "D" strings. To play the notes on the "G" string, it will be necessary to raise the right elbow (bow arm) slightly higher than on the other strings. Also, the left elbow must be held well underneath the violin to play the notes on the "G" string.

SIDE VIEW

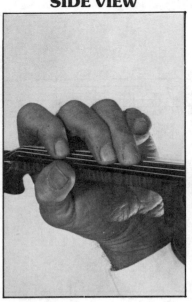

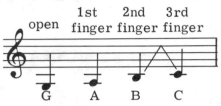

open | 1st finger | 2nd finger | 3rd finger

G A B C

PLAY AND COMPARE

"E" STRING — open, 1st, 2d, 3d — E F# G# A

"A" STRING — open 1st 2d 3d — A B C# D

"D" STRING — open 1st 2d 3d — D E F# G

"G" STRING — open 1st 2d 3d — G A B C

18

3/4 TIME

Up until now we have been playing in $\frac{4}{4}$ time. This is sometimes called "common" time and indicated by "**C**".

In common time we have four full beats to the measure. (one and, two and, three and, four and). In $\frac{3}{4}$ time we have three beats to the measure (one and, two and, three and). A quarter note gets one full beat in $\frac{3}{4}$ time just as it does in $\frac{4}{4}$ time.

Count - 1 and 2 and 3 and 4 and

Count-1 and 2 and 3 and   1 and 2 and 3 and

DOTTED HALF NOTE

Count:1 and 2 and 3 and

A dotted half note gets 3 full counts!

1—2—3

JACOB'S LADDER

BLOW THE MAN DOWN

19

THE TIE

The tie is a curved line that connects one or more notes. When a tie occurs, you hold the note for the combined value of the two notes tied together. You will bow only the first note. The second note is merely held and not bowed.

"TIE" IN 3/4

"TIE" IN 4/4

ENGLISH SONG

EMPEROR WALTZ

Johann Strauss

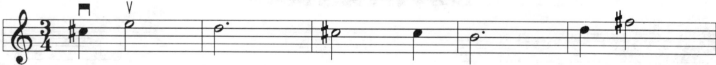

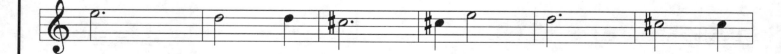

KEY SIGNATURES

For now we should learn a little about "key signatures." When a sharp sign (♯) appears at the beginning of a line,

The sharps indicated will remain sharped throughout the piece. We will not need to write a sharp sign (♯) in front of F and C on the

following songs. The sharp signs will be placed in the "key signature."

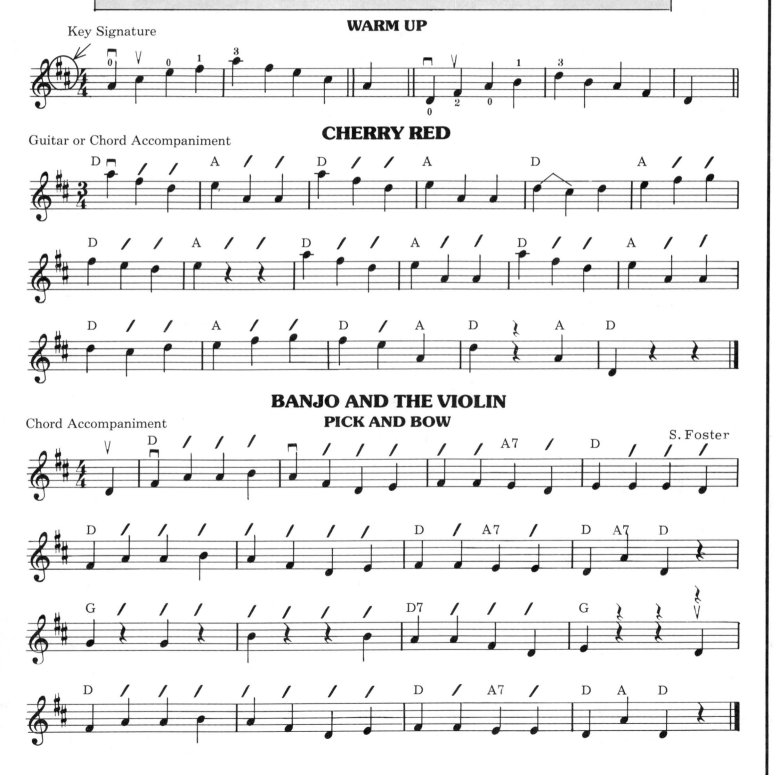

SOLOS

I LIKE BOOGIE

SLEIGH RIDE

TWO STRING BOOGIE

POLKA TIME

MORE ABOUT MUSIC

NOTES ON THE LINES

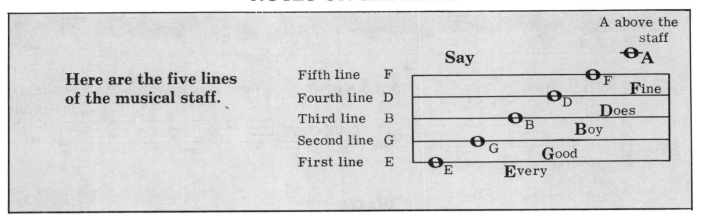

Here are the five lines of the musical staff.

		Say
Fifth line	F	**F**ine
Fourth line	D	**D**oes
Third line	B	**B**oy
Second line	G	**G**ood
First line	E	**E**very

A above the staff

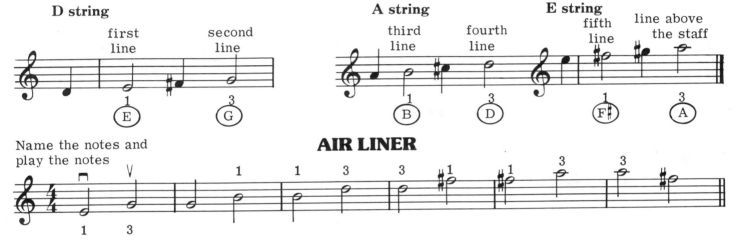

D string — first line (1) E — second line (3) G

A string — third line (1) B — fourth line (3) D

E string — fifth line (1) F♯ — line above the staff (3) A

AIR LINER

Name the notes and play the notes

WHAT'S NEW

Play and say

SIDE BY SIDE

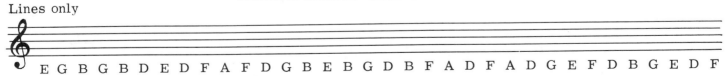

WRITE-READ-SAY-AND PLAY

Lines only

E G B G B D E D F A F D G B E B G D B F A D F A D G E F D B G E D F

Students should continue to write notes on both the lines and spaces. Students who do not write will not learn to read as readily!

23

THE SPACES

Open D-A-E strings plus the second finger on the D-A and E strings give us the names of the spaces.

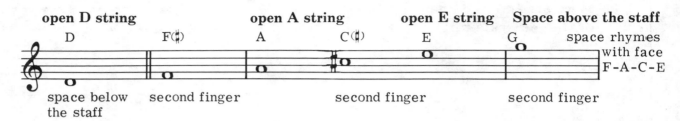

WARM UP

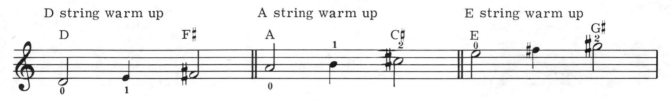

SPACE MOVEMENT #1

SPACE MOVEMENT #2

SIDE BY SIDE

READ-WRITE-SAY-AND PLAY

G E G F♯ D F♯ C♯ A D A G C♯ E F♯ D C♯ F♯ E D G F♯ C A E G F♯ A D

Note: Students should study and memorize the fingerboard. For example, when playing the third finger on the D string (G), what note is across from G on the A string with the third finger? This example should be studied with all the fingers across the fingerboard. Continue to write notes on the lines and spaces. Teachers should explain about the same letter note appearing on different degrees of the staff.

PART TWO

At this point the student should be able to recognize and name the lines and spaces. However, insist on reciting the notes aloud.

Warm up for the D string-say the notes aloud

Warm up for the A string-say the notes aloud

Put them both together and we have a tone ladder or a D major scale!

D SCALE

TEXAS WALTZ

Chord Accompaniment

SWEET BETSY

Chord Accompaniment

use Long Bow Strokes

SOMETHING NEW

Before proceeding, review the D major scale.

ON MY OWN — DUET

Chord Accompaniment

FALLING LEAVES

Chord Accompaniment

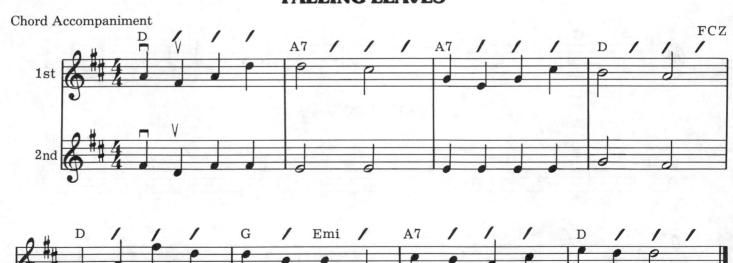

NEW NOTES

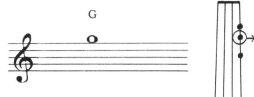
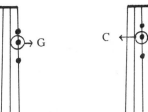
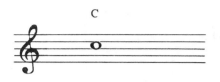

WARM UP

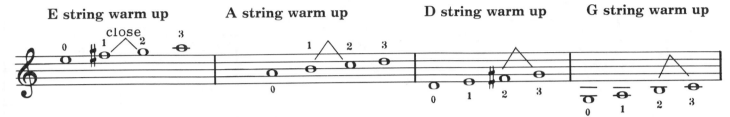

E string warm up   A string warm up   D string warm up   G string warm up

G MAJOR

In the key of G major we have 1 sharp—F♯.
Notice that the position of the fingers and the location of the half steps are the same on the G and D strings and the same on the A and E strings. Study the following music carefully before proceeding.

G SCALE OR G TONE LADDER

OLD MAC'S FARM

CHECK POINT — DIATONIC HALF STEPS

Repeat and memorize

Where are the half steps?
Where are the whole steps?

OPUS

SEGUE NO. 1

FCZ

PART THREE
THE NATURAL SIGN ♮

The distance between F♮ and F♯ is a half step. You will remember that the sign for a half step is ∧. Study the diagram before playing. Check your hand position (elbow well under violin, wrist straight, fingers curled over the E string.)

① Press your 1st finger down on F♯ and play for 4 counts.

② Without raising your finger, slide back to the nut for F♮.

Repeat this movement several times. Try to play F♮ and F♯ in tune.

A natural sign looks like this(♮). It cancels out a sharp.

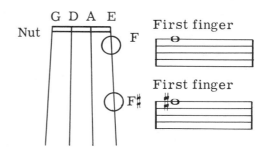

FIRST FINGER STUDY

KEY OF C MAJOR — NO SHARPS

MI TO LA

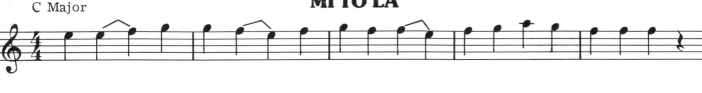

SONG FOR BENNY

THINGS TO REMEMBER

Left arm well under the violin-left wrist straight-fingers well curved over the fingerboard.

THE 16 BASIC NOTES ON THE VIOLIN

KEY OF C MAJOR – FIRST POSITION

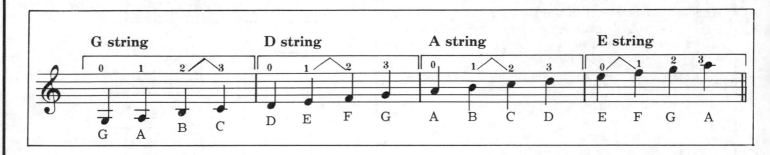

TAKE OFF

Slowly

(use Long Bows)

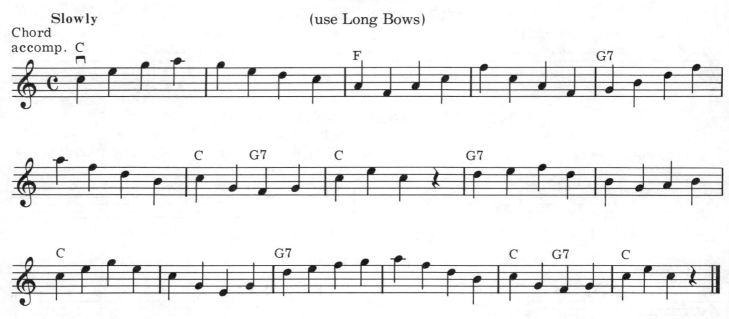

JET FLIGHT

CHECK POINT
A REVIEW OF THE 16 BASIC NOTES

(Insert Alphabet Letters and String Numbers)
1st-string (E) 2nd string (A) 3rd string (D) 4th string (G)

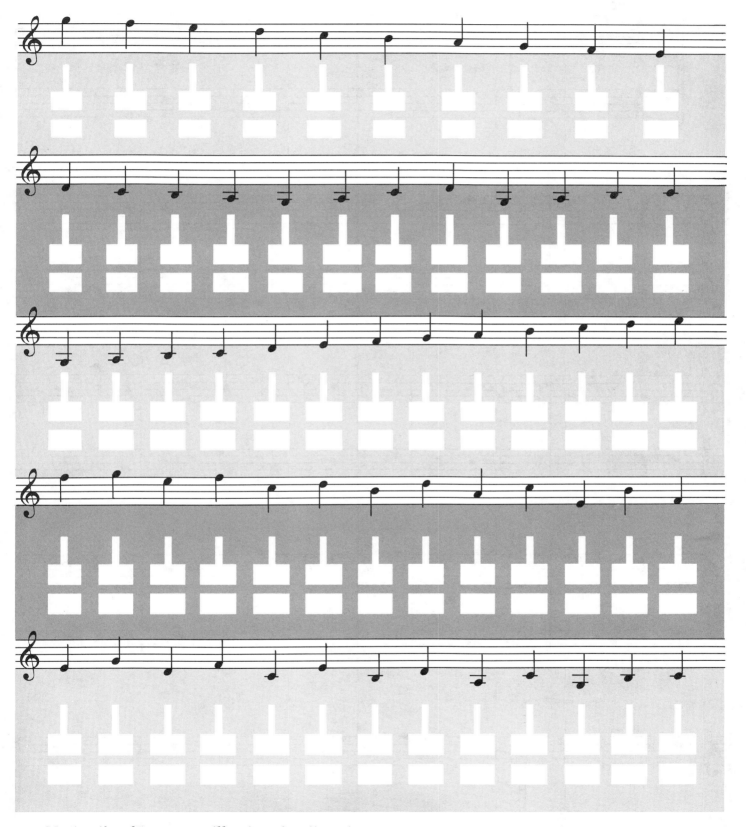

Master the above - we will not review it again.

CONTRA
(FOR TWO VIOLINS)

PIZZICATO
(ABBR. PIZZ.)

Pizzicato as well as tremolo on the violin is credited to Monteverde (+1643). Pizzicato means to pluck the string with the finger (first finger) instead of using the bow.

CHANGING FROM BOWING POSITION TO PIZZICATO POSITION

(Study the Photos Carefully)

Notice photo No. 3.—The position of the first finger. The string should be plucked over the fingerboard and not where the bow travels. Changing from bowing position to pizzicato position should be practiced in four movements, as follows.

①. Starting with up bow play open A string to the frog.   ②. Raise the bow slightly away from the violin (change to photo No. 2).   ③ Place the hand down in position as in photo No. 3.   ④ Pluck the string. This procedure should be practiced on all four strings

MR. MONTEVERDE

✕ Note to the teacher. Students may need further help on the above subjects. Starting with down bow on the above exerises is recomended. When pizz. appears on the music, pluck the strings "pizzicato". "Arco" is an Italian word meaning bow, start bowing.

1ST AND 2ND ENDINGS

This sign (:‖) is a repeat sign. It means to go back to the beginning or to this sign (‖:). When we play a song that has a repeat, we frequently have a first and 2nd ending.

They will be shown like this :

1. The first time through play the 1st ending and repeat back to the beginning.
2. The 2nd time through skip the first ending and play the 2nd ending.

WARM UP FOR CHOPSTICKS

C major scale

Short strokes or try pizzacato on this one

CHOPSTICKS   PART ONE

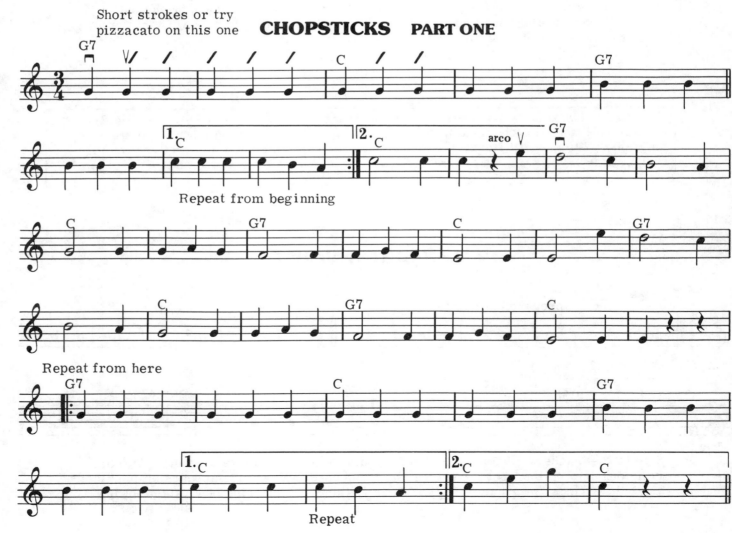

Repeat from beginning

Repeat from here

Repeat

REST REVIEW

The Whole Rest
Whole rests hang down from the fourth line and they receive four full beats.

Half Rest
The Half Rest sits on the third line and it receives two beats.

The Quarter Rest
The quarter rest receives one full count.

RESTS ARE SIGNS OF SILENCE

Find The Mistake and Correct Each Measure.
Each measure must have four full beats.

PLAY, REST, AND COUNT ALOUD

THREE BEATS PER MEASURE

1 2 3

Short strokes or pizzicato

CHOPSTICKS   PART TWO

1.
Repeat from beginning
2.

Repeat from here

1.
Repeat
2.

8TH NOTES

An eighth note gets one half of the time value given to a quarter note. Thus, there are two eighth notes for each quarter note.

Compare the following:

Eighth notes will either look like this (♪) or, when several appear, like this (♫).

Eighth rests will look like this (⅞).

COUNT!

PLAY AND COUNT ALOUD

Eighth notes can be written with a flag ♪ or with a beam ♫. They receive the same time value, and are counted in the same manner.

PICK UP NOTES

The notes at the beginning of a song (before the first measure) are referred to as "pick up notes". The rhythm for the pick up notes is taken from the last measure. Here are some examples.

TONE LADDER USING G AND D STRINGS — G SCALE

RHYTHM SCALE

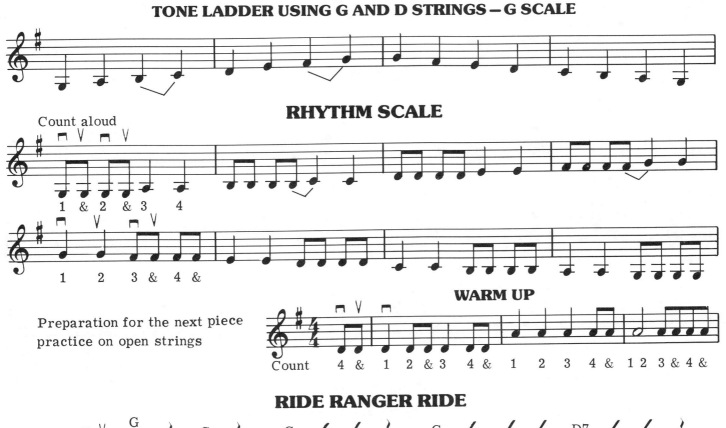

Count aloud

Preparation for the next piece practice on open strings

WARM UP

RIDE RANGER RIDE

JOLLY OLD ST. NICK

37

CLEMENTINE

CAN CAN

WEEPING WILLOW

"A" TONE LADDER

AUNT RHODY'S GOOSE

"G" TONE LADDER

LIBERTY

"C" TONE LADDER

Warm up for The March

MARCH MILITAIRE

F. Schubert

DOWN HOME BOOGIE – IN C

THE FOURTH FINGER

Of the four fingers, the fourth finger is the shortest. It is necessary to have a good position in order to play with the fourth finger. (Left elbow should be held well underneath the violin.) Curve your fingers well above each note. In the following studies, the first finger remains down as marked. Here are some examples.

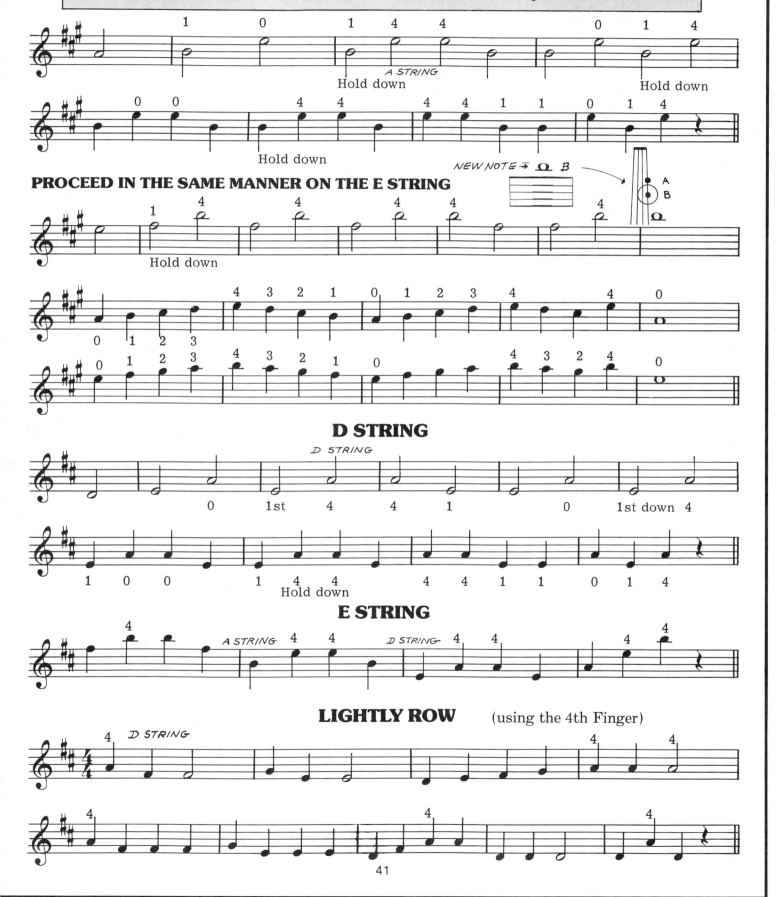

PROCEED IN THE SAME MANNER ON THE E STRING

D STRING

E STRING

LIGHTLY ROW (using the 4th Finger)

41

BOWING STUDIES

SLURRED NOTES

A slur sign can be placed above the notes ♪♪♪ or, it may be placed below the notes ♩♩ . This indicates that they are to be played in one bow. All of the notes must get equal division of the bow. Here are some examples. Remember, it is very important to count while you play. Good bowing means moving only that part of the arm from the elbow down.

One half of bow for each note.

One third of the bow for each note.

Four notes to one bow.

The slur sign applies only to different notes.

OLD JOE CLARK

FURTHER INSTRUCTION ON BOWING

A dot placed above or below two are more notes connected by a slur indicates that they are to be played in one bow, with a short pause between notes. The bow is simply stopped and started again. The bow must remain down on the strings.

BOW STUDIES

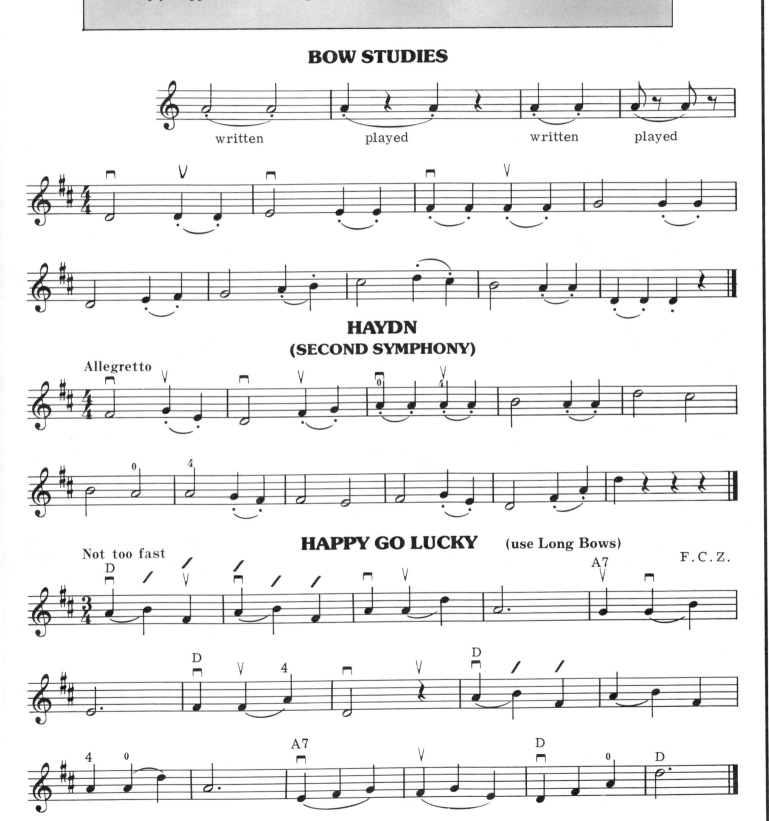

HAYDN
(SECOND SYMPHONY)

HAPPY GO LUCKY (use Long Bows)

STACCATO BOWING

When playing staccato, the notes should be detached, distinct and separated from each other. Use short, quick strokes, no pressure on the bow. Pause between the notes. Staccato notes may be written with the dot above or below the notes.

Example — Dot below   Dot above

With very short strokes in the middle of the bow, play the following examples.

STACCATO BOW STUDY

*segue

STUDY #2

TRAMP — TRAMP — TRAMP

Short heavy strokes

F.C.Z.

* Segue = Continue on in the same manner

44

THE DOTTED QUARTER NOTE

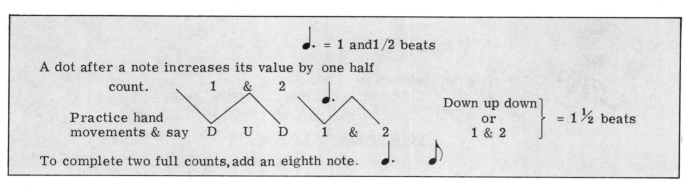

The following examples should be done in three ways:
① Studied
② Counted aloud
③ Play and count aloud

Practice Counting like you practice your violin. Remember, you must be able to count what you play and play what you count.

Here are a few examples of dotted quarter notes and eighth notes. Study them carefully. We cannot review them again.

2/4 TIME

This sign $\frac{2}{4}$ indicates two-four time

2 beats per measure
4 - Type of note receiving one full beat (quarter note).
In Two-Four time, we will have 2 beats per measure.

THE HAPPY FARMER

R. Schumann

MORE RHYTHM PATTERNS

SONG

Foster

DANCE IN G

Violin warm up   Raise 1/2 step

J. Haydn

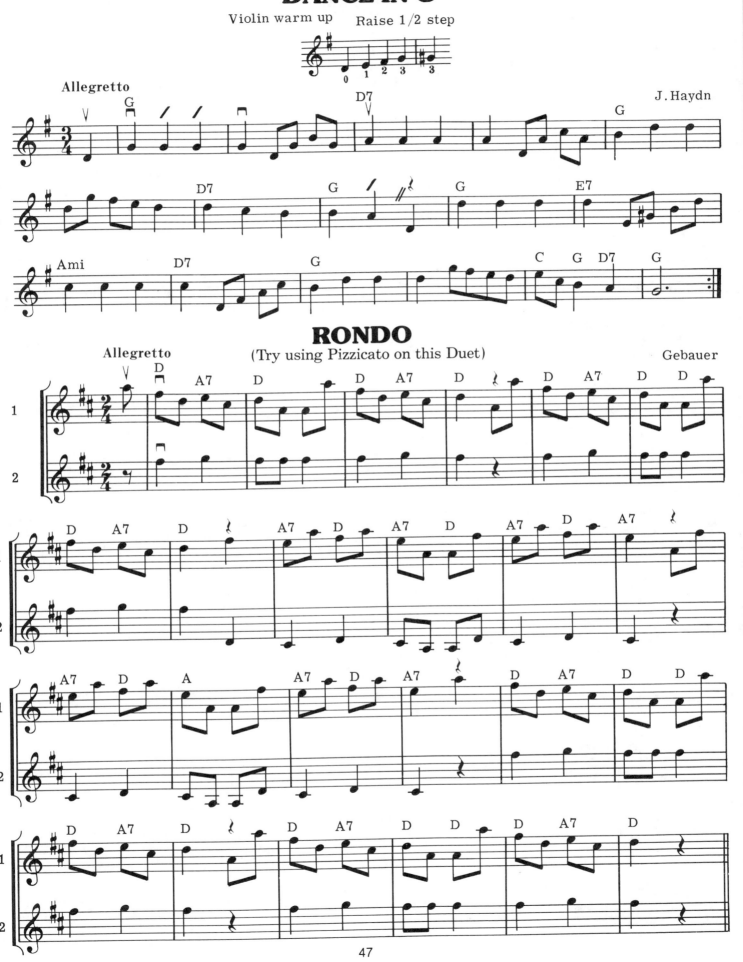

RONDO

(Try using Pizzicato on this Duet)

Gebauer

FLATS

We have already studied sharps. You will remember that a sharp sign (♯) raises the pitch of a note 1/2 step. A flat sign looks like this (♭). A flat lowers the pitch of a note 1/2 step. A natural sign (♮) cancels out a sharp or a flat.

ACCIDENTALS

An accidental is a sharp or flat that does not appear in the key signature. An accidental applies only to that measure in which it appears.

KEY REVIEW — PLAY AND COMPARE

OPEN "A" STRING & FIRST FINGER "B♭"

Preparation for the key of F Major

This position is very close. The first finger must be strongly arched. Study the diagram. Hold the thumb and hand in the normal playing position. This never moves. Only the first finger should slide back and forth. The diagram shows the exact distance from B back to B♭.

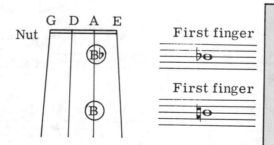

The distance between B flat to B natural is a half step. Study the diagram carefully before playing. Before proceeding, check hand position. (Elbow well under the violin, wrist straight, fingers well curved over A string.) Press first finger down firmly on B-Play for four counts -slight pause-slide first back to nut (B♭)-play for 4 counts -pause. Try to play in good tune. Do not raise first finger when sliding back and forth.

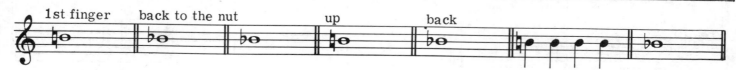

48

CHECK POINT

If the student has not already changed the way the bow is held, this is the appropriate time.

CHANGE BOW

FROM THIS

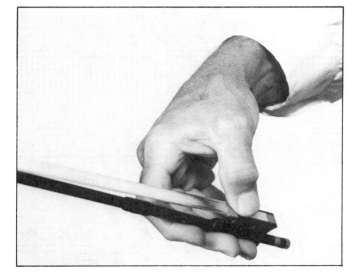

TO THIS

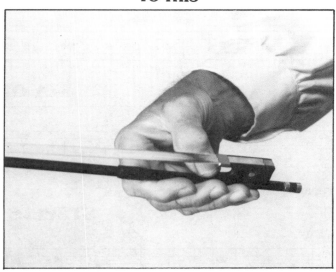

PREPARING THE FIRST FINGER
BACK TO THE NUT

"B"

FIRST FINGER ON THE "A" STRING

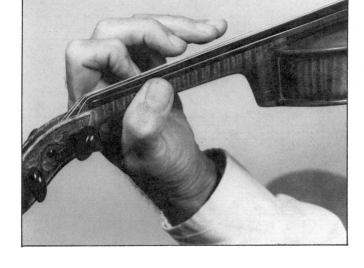

"B♭"

FIRST FINGER ON THE "A" STRING AT THE NUT

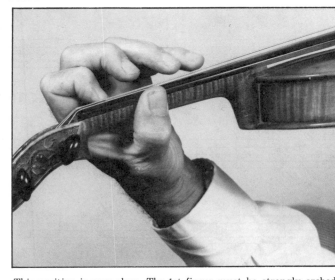

This position is very close. The 1st finger must be strongly arched. Study the picture carefully. Hold the thumb and hand in normal playing position.

When sliding from B back to B♭, do not raise the 1st finger. The thumb should remain stationary. Practice this same position on the E string, going from F♯ to F natural.

49

A NEW KEY SIGNATURE — F MAJOR

(In the Key of F Major we have 1 Flat — B♭)

TONE LADDER WITH B♭

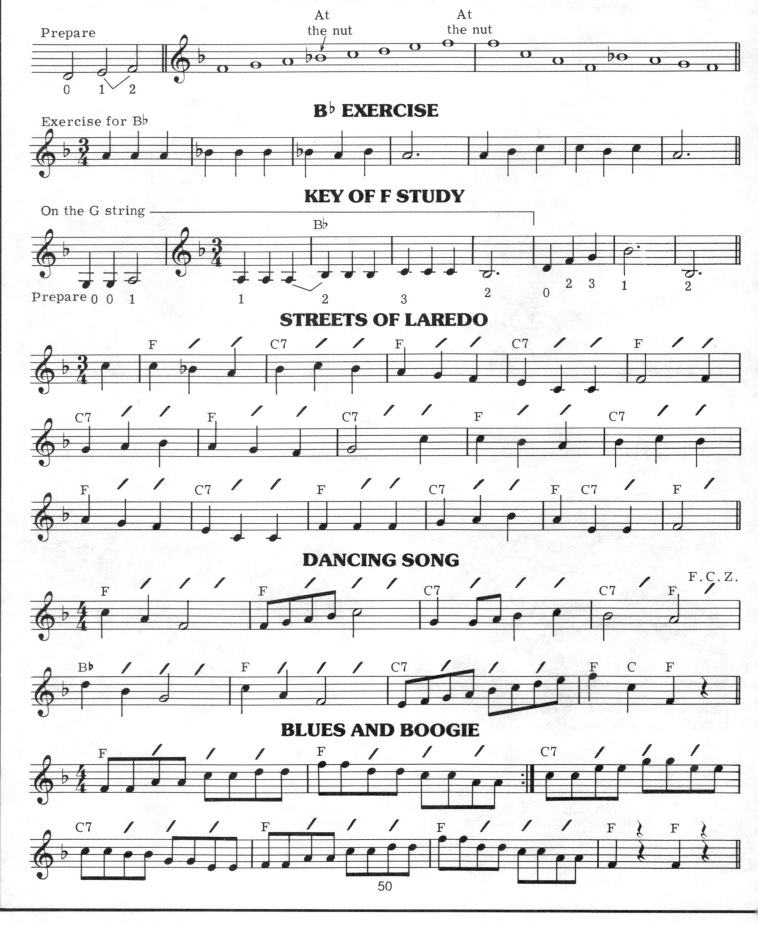

B♭ EXERCISE

KEY OF F STUDY

STREETS OF LAREDO

DANCING SONG

BLUES AND BOOGIE

LEARNING ABOUT HALF STEPS

Two kinds of half steps occur in music-chromatic and diatonic. We will now learn about the chromatic half step-when doing examples-B-C-D-E, do not raise the second or third fingers when sliding up. Listen carefully for the correct pitch.

HERE ARE SOME EXAMPLES

(ON THE D STRING — GOING UP)

ON THE A STRING

CHROMATIC WALTZ

51

TRIPLETS
(THREE OF A KIND)

Play them the way you say them.

Count aloud, clap the hands or tap on the music stand saying.

1 tri—plet 2 tri—plet 3 tri—plet

A Group of three notes played to the time of one quarter note

TRIPLET DUET

Not too fast

Mel Bay

TRIPLET STUDY

Possible paterns

Note: Students should be constantly reminded about the hand & arm positions, short fingernails, and counting aloud. The parts on the above triplet study should be alternated.

TRIPLE PLAY

Bow Markings have been simplified and arranged to further improve right arm motion.

Mel Bay

MARCH OF THE GIANTS

SIXTEENTH NOTES
(FOUR OF A KIND)

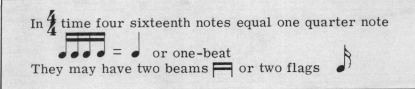

Count them the way you say them.

1 sixteenth note   2 sixteenth note   3 sixteenth note   4 sixteenth note

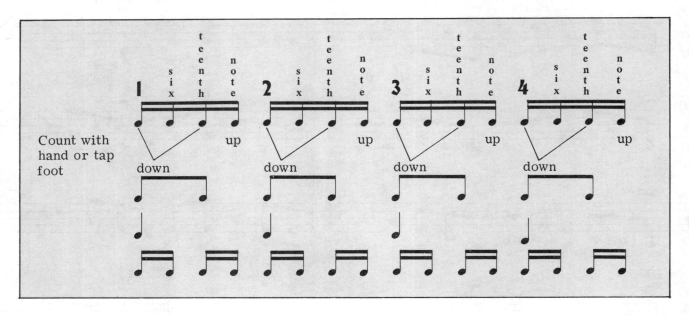

TABLE OF NOTES AND RESTS

Whole note	o	Whole measure rest
Half note		A half rest
Quarter notes		A quarter, rest
Eight notes		An eight rest
Sixteenth notes		A sixteenth rest

* Counting down and up with the hand plus singing the name of the notes aloud in the correct time and pitch is a type of solfeggio, taught in Italy.
Remember-you only play as well as you count.   Practice counting frequently!

MORE ABOUT SIXTEENTH NOTES

Study the above carefully · we will not again review it.

SIXTEENTH NOTE STUDIES

NEW RHYTHM

When an eighth note is followed by two 16th notes,  they may be counted in this manner.

Count: One note on the down beat and two notes on the up beat

When properly done (the down and up movment) the eighth note will be counted or played on the down beat, the two sixteenth notes on the up beat. Remember, keep a steady down and up hand movement.

RHYTHM STUDY

ETUDE #1

ETUDE #2

56

ANOTHER NEW RHYTHM

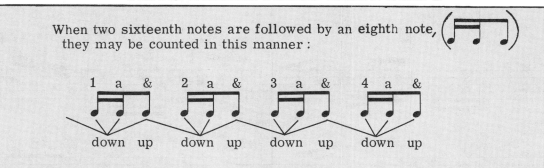

When two sixteenth notes are followed by an **eighth note,** they may be counted in this manner :

1 a & 2 a & 3 a & 4 a &

down up down up down up down up

The above rhythm is the exact opposite of page 54.
Here we have two sixteenth on the down beat and the eighth note on the up beat.

RHYTHM STUDY

count aloud

1 a & 2 a &

SCALING

short strokes

1 a & 2 a &

STAMPEDE

Middle of the bow
Lively

CHECK POINT

FLOP EARED MULE

TURKISH MARCH

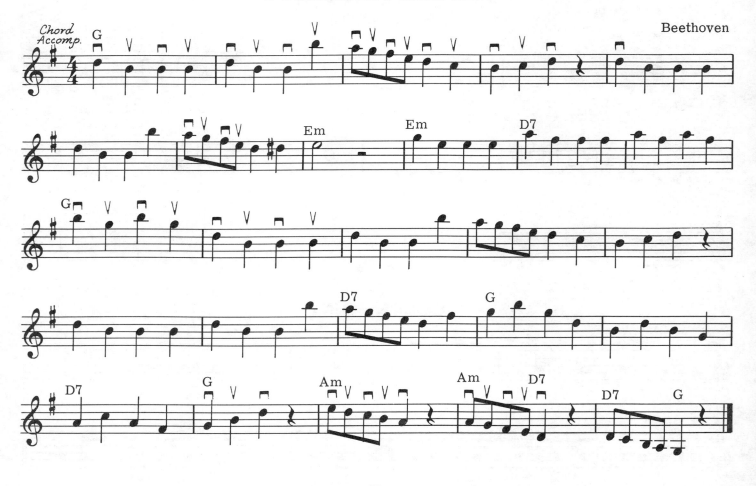

58

EXTRA PLAYING STUDIES
SONATA (THEMES)

PIZZICATO POLKA

THE THIRD AND FOURTH FINGERS

Dropping the third and fourth fingers down and away from the fingerboard (when playing) seems to be a common, but serious, problem for some students. The following exercises are especially written to help the student concentrate on keeping the fingers over the fingerboard. With the left elbow well under the violin, and fingers remaining directly over the strings and fingerboard, play the following studies. Slowly increase the speed at your own convenience. These exercises should be practiced daily and remember to keep the fingers over the fingerboard at all times. Using the fourth finger as much as possible can also be a great help in maintaining a good hand position.

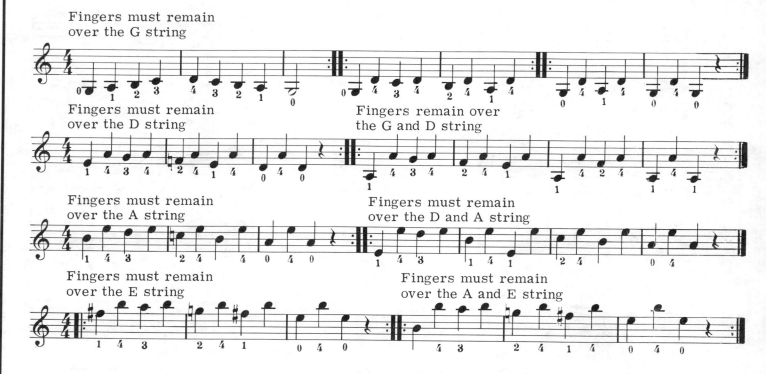

VIRTUOSO STUDY

The fourth finger remains down on the D string when playing on the G string

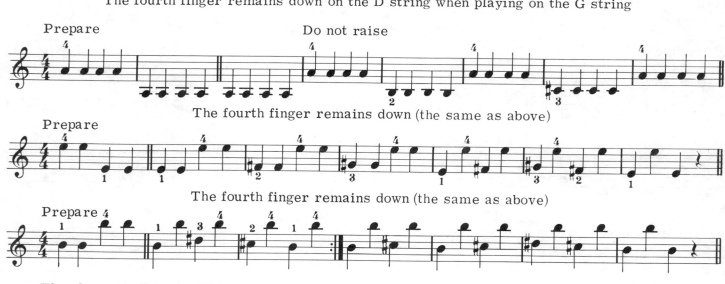

The above studies should be practiced daily as a disciplinary drill for keeping the fingers over the fingerboard.

DEVELOPING A FLEXIBLE WRIST

Place the bow on the G string; the hand and elbow at the proper height for playing on both the G and D strings. Play the G string for three counts. Pause at the rest, without moving the elbow, drop the hand and play the D string for three counts. The bow should be drawn in an even, steady manner. The bow hair should remain flat on the strings. Do not turn hand from side to side.

IN THE SAME MANNER ON THE D AND A STRINGS

IN THE SAME MANNER ON THE A AND E STRINGS

SMOOTH SAILING

F. C. Z.

BOWING THE TONE LADDER

FURTHER INSTRUCTION ON BOWING

To produce a good, clear tone, the bow should be moved in a straight line parallel to the bridge. The right elbow should be held low, except when passing down to the G string, when you may raise it slightly. The following studies should be executed from the middle to the tip of the bow. The wrist should be loose and relaxed and move only that part of the right arm from the elbow down.

ETUDE NO. 1

ETUDE NO. 2

STACCATO

Staccato-An Italian word meaning short, detached notes. The following may be practiced on the D string at the middle of the bow. With sufficient resin on the bow, the hair not too tight, about one-half inch from the stick, the elbow slightly lower than the wrist, make a short stroke with the wrist and at the same time press the stick down slightly with the index finger biting into the string. At the end of the stroke, let up on the bow. This procedure may be done the same, up bow or down bow. A dot placed above or below a note indicates staccato.

HERE ARE SOME EXAMPLES

The following examples should be practiced separately and not in sequence.

63

MORE ABOUT STACCATO

GAVOTTE

64

SYNCOPATION: A HIDDEN BEAT

Here are some examples:

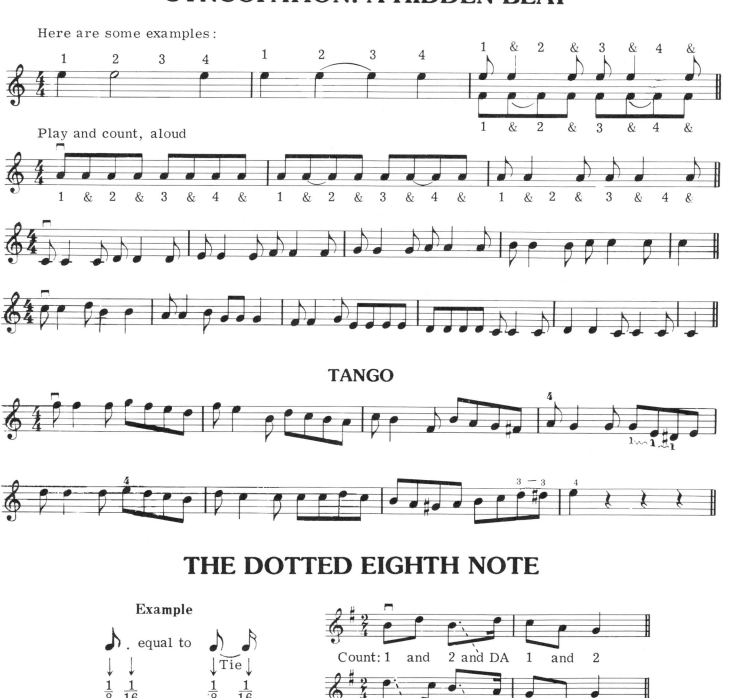

TANGO

THE DOTTED EIGHTH NOTE

MORE ABOUT THE DOTTED EIGHTH AND SIXTEENTH NOTES

Prepare

Segue

THE DOTTED EIGHTH AND SIXTEENTH (CONTINUED)

The following studies should be played in the middle of the bow with little or no pressure. The bow must remain down on the strings, the elbow at the proper height and a good, flexible wrist.

COUNTRY GARDENS

English

Moderato

MARCH-TIME

Segue

Fine

D.C. al Fine

66

PRACTICING SCALES

Good practice habits are surely the quickest and easiest way to becoming a good player. A good daily routine and the desire to learn are important. Before playing any piece or exercise, practice the major scale and the two relative minors. EXAMPLE. In the Key of C Major, practice the C scale and the A melodic and harmonic minors. They should be played ascending and descending in their particular forms. At this level, they may be played two octaves when not going beyond the First Position. Here are some abbreviated examples.

Related scales have the same key signature. Unitonic scales have the same tonic.

COMBINED SCALE AND BOWING DRILLS

Scales in all keys may be practiced on three different parts of the bow: (1) middle of the bow, (2) upper part of the bow and (3) lower part of the bow. The wrist should be relaxed and remember that moving the part of the right arm from the elbow down will be a great help in achieving a flexible wrist.

MORE ABOUT BOWING

At a slow tempo, the following scale should be practiced in this manner. Starting with a down bow, play the quarter note to the tip. eight notes at the tip. Long bow the eighth notes at the frog. Here are some examples.

CHECK POINT

The elbow should be held higher when playing on the G string and will drop slightly when changing from G, D and E strings. Strive for a loose and flexible wrist.

SIXTEEN PIECES IN DIFFERENT KEYS

Preceded by the major scales, their relative minors, and broken chords.

SOLDIERS ON PARADE

Jessel

A MINOR
RELATIVE MINOR TO C MAJOR

To establish a relationship, it is necessary to employ two subjects. In music we use the terms "major" and "minor". All scales or pieces that have the same key signature are related. This rule applies to any key signature.

A melodic minor: The 6th and 7th degrees are raised ascending, lowered descending.

A Harmonic minor: The 7th degree is raised ascending and descending.

GRANDIOSO

Andantino (Big bows)

F. C. Z.

G MAJOR

MINUET NO. 2

J.S.Bach

E MINOR

G major and E minor are related [one sharp (F♯ sharp) in the key signature]

THE LONELY BOATMAN

CHECK POINT

Scales should be practiced every day with the different rhythm patterns. (See page 10.)

D MAJOR

CONCERTO NO. 5

Seitz.

B MINOR
RELATIVE OF D MAJOR

B Melodic minor

B Harmonic minor

CONCERTO NO. 5 WITH VARIATION

Seitz.
F. C. Z.

A MAJOR

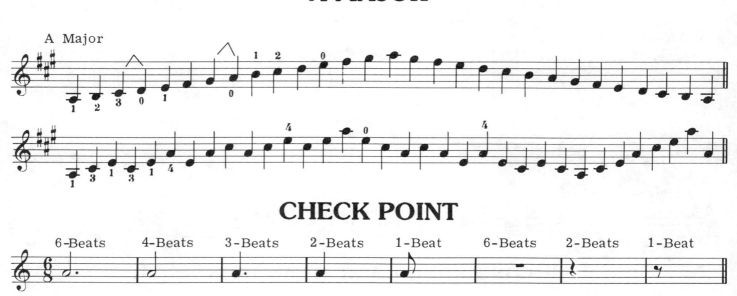

CHECK POINT

TARANTELLA

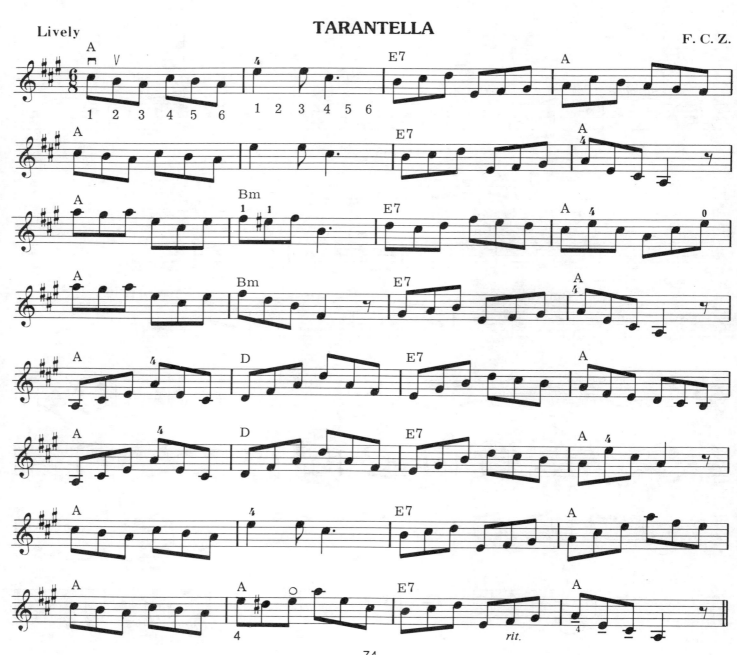

F# MAJOR
RELATED TO A MAJOR

SICIALIA-BELLA

E MAJOR

NORWEGIAN DANCE

Grieg

C♯ MINOR
RELATED TO E MAJOR

C♯ Melodic Minor

Extension

For better intonation
first finger may remain down

up first finger

C♯ Harmonic Minor

Extension

RUSSIAN SAILORS

Vivo

HUNGARIAN TUNE

Bartok

Andante

F MAJOR

F Major Scale

Extension

CHILDHOOD FANTASY

Andante

Mozart

FREULICH

Allegretto

Beethoven

D MINOR
RELATED TO F MAJOR

MINUET IN D MINOR

Andantino

Bach

B♭ MAJOR

NO SAGGIO

Allegretto

F. C. Z.

G MINOR
RELATED TO B♭ MAJOR

G Melodic Minor

G Harmonic Minor

MOLTO-MINORE

E♭ MAJOR

E♭ Major Scale

Extension

BEN-HUR
MARCH

Paull

Tempo di marcia

C MINOR
RELATED TO E♭ MAJOR

FIFTH SYMPHONY

Beethoven

A♭ MAJOR

A♭ Major Scale

BEL-CANTO

Andante-broadly

F. C. Z.

F MINOR
RELATED TO A♭ MAJOR

VILLA-ROSSA

DUET IN D MINOR

Violin Duet

THEME AND VARIATIONS

Paganini

VARIATION NO. 1

Hammer the strings with the fingers, especially the fourth finger. Change from string to string without accent... a good, flexible wrist.

VARIATION NO. 2

VARIATION NO. 3

G MINOR SYMPHONY NO. 40

RUBBER NECK RAG

SEGUE

Cantante quasi cadenza

F. C. Z.

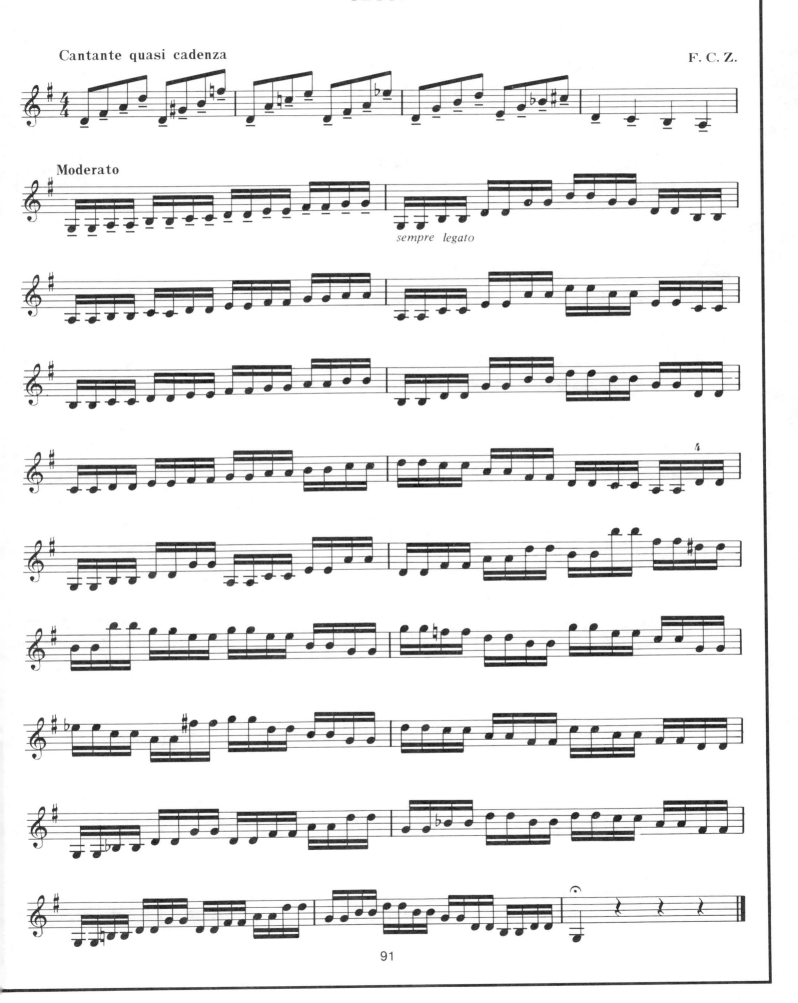

Moderato

sempre legato

91

FISHERS HORNPIPE

CHICKEN REEL

STACCATINO
MIDDLE OF THE BOW

F. C. Z.

MAJOR AND MINOR

F. C. Z.

CANZONE-AMOROSA
FROM *A DAY IN VENICE*

E. Nevin

ALA-PAGANINI

* A Major and F#Minor Scles

The following tune is to be executed with wrist movement only. Play at the middle of the bow. The forearm and elbow should remain still with little or no movement except when passing from one string to another. Work for a good, flexible wrist.

HI JO
POLKA

B♭Major and G Minor Scales

INTRODUCING THE THIRD POSITION

Playing in the positions means shifting the hand to a higher position on the neck. EXAMPLE: On the G string, playing the note A with the first finger; that is the First Position, the note B with the first finger; that is the Second Position, and the note C with the first finger; that is the Third Position. Memorizing this sequence of notes and fingerings on each string can be a great help in learning the positions. The purpose of playing in the positions is to extend the range of the Violin. Students who do not play in the positions must remain in elementary music and may never advance to playing First Violin.

PREPARING THE HAND

A good hand position; elbow well under the violin, the thumb opposite the first joint of the first finger, the opening between the base of the thumb and the neck, the wrist straight and fingers directly over the string. Moving only that part of the arm from the elbow up, slowly slide the hand up and back the fingerboard (as a preparatory movement) several times.

PLAYING THE THIRD POSITION (ON THE G STRING)

The first finger replacing the third finger on the note C

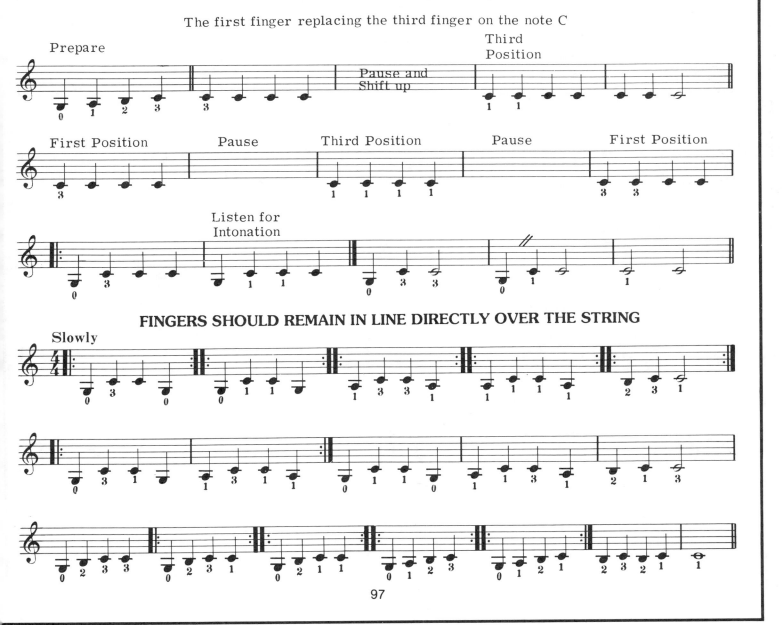

FINGERS SHOULD REMAIN IN LINE DIRECTLY OVER THE STRING

THIRD POSITION ON THE G STRING (CONTINUED)

G-STRING SOLO

TWISTER

CHANGING POSITIONS WITH THE SECOND FINGER

CHANGING POSITIONS WITH THE THIRD FINGER

CHANGING POSITIONS WITH THE FOURTH FINGER

CHECK POINT

Elbow well under the violin. A good hand position; fingers well rounded in a straight line directly over the strings, finger remaining on the string when changing position. Listen for intonation; tune the violin as often as possible.

THE THIRD POSITION ON THE D STRING

The position of the notes and the fingers are the same as on the G string, only the names of the notes change.

THE FINGERS SHOULD REMAIN IN LINE DIRECTLY OVER THE STRING

TONE LADDER

D-STRING SOLO

99

TWISTER

PLAY AND COMPARE NO. 1

PLAY AND COMPARE NO. 2

TEXAS WALTZ

Mel Bay

CHANGING POSITIONS WITH THE SECOND FINGER

CHANGING POSITIONS WITH THE THIRD FINGER

CHANGING POSITIONS WITH THE FOURTH FINGER

THE THIRD POSITION ON THE A STRING

The position of the notes and the fingers are the same as on the G and D strings: only the names of the notes are different.

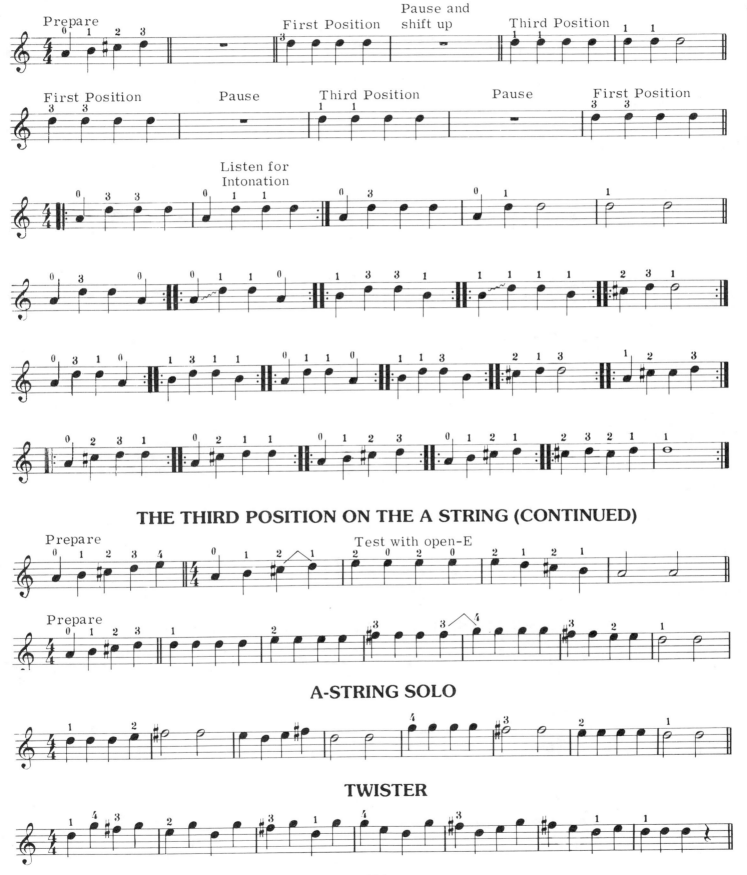

THE THIRD POSITION ON THE A STRING (CONTINUED)

A-STRING SOLO

TWISTER

CHANGING POSITIONS WITH THE SECOND FINGER

CHANGING POSITIONS WITH THE THIRD FINGER

CHANGING POSITIONS WITH THE FOURTH FINGER

THE THIRD POSITION ON THE E STRING

The position of the notes and the fingers are the same as on the G, D and A strings; only the names of the notes are different.

FINGERS SHOULD REMAIN IN LINE DIRECTLY OVER THE STRING

THE THIRD POSITION ON THE E STRING (CONTINUED)

Changing positions with the second finger

E-STRING SOLO

Two new notes in the third position on the E string

High C♯
Third finger

High D
Fourth finger

E-STRING SOLO

TWISTER

CHANGING POSITIONS WITH THE THIRD FINGER

CHANGING POSITIONS WITH THE FOURTH FINGER

THE SIXTEEN PRINCIPLE NOTES IN THE THIRD POSITION

TEXAS WALTZ — A AND D STRINGS

Andante (long bows)

Play and compare with the above

TEXAS WALTZ — E AND A STRINGS

CHECK POINT

Memorizing the notes, that are across from each other on different strings with the same fingering, could be a great help in learning the Third Position. Left elbow well under the violin, fingers well rounded over the strings, tune the violin often and keep fingernails short.

Students may find the five following short pieces more of a challenge. They have been purposely written in this manner to give the student a better understanding of the Third Position.

ROBIN HOOD

ANDY THE DANDY

BOSCO THOMPSON

F. C. Z.

Certificate of Completion

This is to certify that

_____

STUDENT'S NAME

has successfully completed Mel Bay's Violin Method.

_____

TEACHER'S NAME

_____

DATE